Original title:
The Continuum of Connection

Copyright © 2024 Swan Charm
All rights reserved.

Author: Paula Raudsepp
ISBN HARDBACK: 978-9916-86-587-3
ISBN PAPERBACK: 978-9916-86-588-0
ISBN EBOOK: 978-9916-86-589-7

A Tapestry of Souls

In the quiet night we weave,
Threads of dreams we believe.
Colors bright and shadows deep,
In our hearts, the echoes seep.

Stories shared, entwined in time,
A dance of fate, a subtle rhyme.
Binding us with gentle grace,
In this sacred, boundless space.

Silent whispers, hands that clasp,
Moments fleeting, memories grasp.
A tapestry, both new and old,
Each shared heart, a tale retold.

Through the storm, through the night,
Together, we seek the light.
In the tapestry, we find our role,
For we are, indeed, a tapestry of souls.

Synapses of Serenity

In the stillness, neurons spark,
Through the calm, we find our mark.
Peaceful thoughts, like rivers flow,
In quiet moments, wisdom grows.

With each breath, a journey starts,
Synapses dance within our hearts.
Harmony in subtle ways,
Guiding us through hazy days.

Nature whispers in the breeze,
With each sigh, our worries cease.
A gentle touch, a knowing glance,
In this embrace, we find our chance.

Collective dreams softly rise,
Underneath the endless skies.
Together in this sacred space,
We reach for joy, our souls interlace.

The Melody of Togetherness

A symphony of hearts collide,
In harmony, we take our stride.
Notes like laughter fill the air,
Each moment cherished, rare and fair.

Voices blend, a perfect tune,
Underneath the glowing moon.
In our laughter, we find release,
Together, we discover peace.

Through the trials, through the strife,
Music becomes a way of life.
In every chorus, love we find,
A melody that's intertwined.

The dance of souls in perfect time,
Creates a rhythm, a gentle chime.
In the heart's embrace, we sing,
Celebrating what togetherness can bring.

Interwoven Paths

Life's journey twists and turns,
In every heart, a fire burns.
Paths that cross, just like the stars,
Each in-depth, collective scars.

Through the forests, valleys wide,
We walk together, side by side.
In the silence, stories told,
Through the young and through the old.

Whispers echo in the night,
Guided by a shared insight.
Every step, a lesson learned,
In the tapestry, hope is earned.

In the weave of joy and pain,
We find ourselves, like summer rain.
Interwoven, hand in hand,
Together, we explore this land.

Cosmic Threads of Unity

In the vastness, stars collide,
A dance of light, where dreams abide.
Galaxies spin in graceful flow,
Bound by threads we do not know.

Whispers echo from the night,
Guiding hearts towards what's right.
Together, we weave our fate,
In cosmic arms, we resonate.

Beyond the void, a spark ignites,
Illuminating endless nights.
Each pulse a promise, strong and true,
In every soul, a part of you.

Harmony in Dissonance

Notes collide in wild embrace,
A tapestry of sound we trace.
In chaos, beauty finds its way,
A song that guides both night and day.

Rhythms clash and then align,
Creating art so pure, divine.
In discord, voices join as one,
A symphony that's just begun.

Life's melody has shades unclear,
Yet harmony dwells, always near.
Through trials, joy may seem askew,
In every note, a truth rings true.

Serendipitous Encounters

Paths entwine in fleeting grace,
Each meeting stars' designed embrace.
A smile, a glance, a moment shared,
In life's design, we are prepared.

Strangers weave their stories tight,
In cafés, parks, or late at night.
An accidental brush, a chance,
Creates connections in a dance.

Fate guides us, uncertain yet bright,
With every glance, the world feels right.
In laughter and tears, we find delight,
Serendipity's magic in our sight.

Mosaics of Memory

Fragments shine in faded light,
Each piece a story, pure and bright.
Collected whispers of the past,
In every heart, a die is cast.

Snapshots pinned to walls of time,
Moments captured, sweet and sublime.
Laughter echoes, shadows play,
In memory's arms, we find our way.

Colors blend, a vivid hue,
Every heart holds tales anew.
In the mosaic, we find our grace,
Linked forever in time and space.

Eternal Cadence of Life's Symphony

In the hush of dawn's embrace,
Melodies of time take flight,
Nature's whispers blend in grace,
Each heartbeat sings of light.

Winds carry tales untold,
Harmonies of joy and strife,
Through valleys deep and bold,
A dance that maps our life.

Stars twinkle in the night,
Guiding dreams with their glow,
In the silence, pure delight,
Echoes through the ebb and flow.

Raindrops fall, a soft refrain,
Caressing earth with care,
In their rhythm, love remains,
A symphony we all share.

As seasons change and shift,
Life's cadence plays anew,
With each gift, we find our rift,
In melodies, I find you.

Celestial Bonds Stitched with Gratitude

Underneath the vast expanse,
Connections spark and bind,
In every glance, a chance,
To cherish what's enshrined.

Roots entwined, hearts aligned,
Together we rise and stand,
In gratitude, love defined,
Across this wondrous land.

Moments shared, like stardust,
Twinkling bright, never lost,
In this journey, built on trust,
We embrace whatever's tossed.

The gentle hands of fate,
Stitch our stories with care,
In unity, we create,
A fabric rich and rare.

With every dawn that breaks,
We weave our tales anew,
In gratitude, love awakes,
Celestial bonds hold true.

Embraced by the Universe's Arms

In the cradle of the night,
Stars embrace with tender light,
Whispers of the cosmic song,
In their arms, we all belong.

Galaxies swirl, dance in grace,
Time and space, an endless chase,
In their vastness, we find home,
Never more shall we roam alone.

Planets spin in perfect tune,
Chasing dreams beneath the moon,
With each breath, the heavens sigh,
In their love, we learn to fly.

Through stardust trails we wander,
Synchronized with cosmic wonder,
Each heartbeat, a pulse divine,
In the universe, our spirits shine.

Embraced within this grand design,
Life's essence, a sacred sign,
In unity, we rise and charm,
Embraced by the universe's arms.

Luminous Ties

Beneath the stars, we shine so bright,
A bond that glows, a guiding light.
In shadows cast, we find our way,
Together, we dance, come what may.

With every laugh, our joys align,
In whispered dreams, our hopes entwine.
Through trials faced, our spirits soar,
Luminous ties forevermore.

Each moment shared, a treasure rare,
In tapestry woven, we lay bare.
Through stormy nights, or skies so clear,
Our love, a flame, will persevere.

In quiet nights, when silence speaks,
Our hearts converse, the truth it seeks.
In gentle hues of dusk's embrace,
We find a home, our sacred space.

So let us walk this path as one,
With every dawn, new dreams begun.
In every tear, in every sigh,
Our luminous ties will never die.

Constellations of Companionship

In the night sky, bonds appear,
Stars that twinkle, drawing near.
Mapped by stories, fields of dreams,
Constellations burst at the seams.

Each star a friend, with tales to share,
In laughter's glow and heartfelt care.
Together we traverse the phases,
Brightest souls in all the mazes.

Guided by light, we roam so free,
Creating paths of harmony.
In every embrace, we spark a flare,
In the cosmic dance, love lays bare.

Through darkest hours, we find the way,
In constellations, come what may.
Our journeys weave, a celestial art,
Companion stars, a beating heart.

Each moment a wish, igniting dreams,
In the starlit sky, our bond redeems.
As time unfolds, still we will shine,
In constellations forever aligned.

A Journey Through Synergy

In harmony's embrace, we begin,
A journey painted deep within.
Hand in hand, we carve our fate,
Within this dance, we resonate.

With open minds, and hearts so true,
We explore the world, me and you.
Through valleys low, and mountains high,
Together, we touch the sky.

In every lesson, we grow strong,
Together we find where we belong.
With open arms, we face the storm,
In synergy, our hearts stay warm.

Every whisper, a guiding song,
In this adventure, we both belong.
Through laughter's echo, and silence deep,
In this bond, our dreams we keep.

A journey forged in trust and light,
With you, my love, the world feels right.
In every step, our spirits free,
Together in life's sweet synergy.

Resonance of Hearts

In the quiet hum of the night,
Our hearts align, a perfect sight.
In gentle rhythms, we find our grace,
A melody shared in this space.

Through whispers soft, in the moon's glow,
The resonance of love does grow.
In every beat, our lives entwined,
A symphony of hearts combined.

With every tear, a note we play,
In joy and sorrow, come what may.
In harmony pure, we rise and fall,
In love's embrace, we have it all.

Through trials faced, and victories sweet,
The rhythm of life, we greet.
Each chapter penned, with grace and art,
In this sweet world, a resonance of hearts.

As seasons turn, and moments pass,
Our love resounds like shimmering glass.
With every dawn, our song restarts,
Bound together, in resonance, our hearts.

Waves of Affection

Gentle whispers on the shore,
Embracing moments, feeling more.
Crashing tides, the heart's delight,
In the dusk, love ignites.

Dancing shadows in the light,
Every heartbeat feels so right.
Carried forth by ocean's song,
Together, where we belong.

Waves that pull, waves that play,
In your arms, I wish to stay.
Salty air, and laughter free,
In this tide, just you and me.

Forever spun in nature's dance,
In every wave, a fleeting glance.
Ride the swells, embrace the flow,
Waves of love, forever grow.

Chains of Shared Experience

Invisible links, strong and tight,
Binding souls with pure delight.
Moments shared, no words required,
In every glance, our hearts inspired.

Stories woven, threads of gold,
Together we brave, together bold.
From laughter loud to silent cries,
In every truth, our spirit flies.

Pieces gathered, moments sewn,
In this fabric, love is grown.
Through trials faced, and joys amassed,
From every memory, the die is cast.

In the echoes of our past,
We find the strength that holds us fast.
In the tapestry of 'we',
Chains of life set us free.

Ties in the Silence

Between the words, a bond unseen,
In quiet moments, love's serene.
Comfort found in the stillness shared,
A connection deep, a heart laid bare.

No need for noise, no need for sound,
In gentle pauses, joy is found.
With just a look, a knowing smile,
We journey together, mile by mile.

In the hush, our laughter swells,
Unspoken stories, endless spells.
Every heartbeat softly speaks,
In the silence, love uniquely peeks.

Through sunsets watched, and stars aligned,
In tranquil moments, our souls entwined.
In the softest of sighs, a sign,
Ties in the silence, hearts combine.

Connections in the Cosmos

Stars align in patterns wide,
Unseen forces, we can't hide.
Galaxies swirl, a dance of fate,
In this vastness, love's innate.

Planets whisper secrets old,
Stories of hearts, forever bold.
In the starlit skies, dreams take flight,
Illuminating paths of light.

Constellations trace our tale,
With every bump, we will not fail.
A cosmic bond, mysterious, bright,
In the universe, we claim our might.

Through the dark, we find our way,
Guided by stars that softly sway.
Connections deep, where souls converge,
In this cosmos, love's sweet surge.

Ripples in the Water.

Gentle waves caress the shore,
Whispers of secrets, tales of yore.
Each stone tossed, a tremor cast,
Reflecting moments, fading fast.

Sunlight dances on the blue,
Every ripple tells a clue.
Nature sighs in quiet grace,
Time slowed down, an endless space.

Breezes carry laughter's sound,
In the depths, silence found.
Fish weave through, a fleeting glimpse,
Life's ballet in quiet leaps.

Moonlit nights invite the dream,
Stars reflect upon the stream.
Ripples whisper, soft and light,
Carrying wishes into the night.

Every droplet holds a tale,
Of journeys vast, of winds that sail.
In this dance, we find our place,
Ripples in time, a warm embrace.

Ebb and Flow of Souls

Tides of life, they rise and fall,
Echoes lingering, a distant call.
In the currents, we drift and sway,
Chasing shadows, night and day.

Hearts entwined in silent lore,
What once was lost returns once more.
In the silence, stories blend,
Fading moments, time's close friend.

Waves crash loud, then softly sigh,
As spirits soar and then comply.
With each heartbeat, life's refrain,
Ebb and flow, love's sweet gain.

In the stillness, voices blend,
A sacred space where souls transcend.
Together woven, bright and whole,
In this rhythm, we find our role.

As daylight fades, we seek the glow,
Embracing dreams, we ebb and flow.
In the dance of dusk and dawn,
The cycle lives, we carry on.

Threads Weaving in Silence

In the quiet, threads are spun,
Stories woven, one by one.
Each strand a whisper, soft and true,
Binding hearts like morning dew.

Silken fibers glide and curve,
Weaving patterns, the soul's reserve.
With every twist, a memory found,
Silent moments wrap around.

Underneath a starry sky,
Threads connect as dreams comply.
In the stillness, colors blend,
Weaving futures, around the bend.

Time may fray, yet bonds hold tight,
Guiding us through day and night.
In the tapestry of life we spin,
Threads of hope where love begins.

Each needle pricks, a gentle pain,
Yet from the hurt, we rise again.
Together we create this art,
Threads weaving ever, heart to heart.

Echoes Across Time

Voices linger on the breeze,
Carried forth with mighty ease.
In the stillness, whispers play,
Echoes from a distant day.

Mountains stand as witnesses proud,
Holding secrets safe, uncowed.
Through valleys deep, the sounds will flow,
Binding places we come to know.

From ancient stones to skies above,
Every echo tells of love.
In the twilight, shadows blend,
Time's embrace, it has no end.

Moments freeze as echoes call,
Reflections caught on history's wall.
Memories surfacing like a chime,
Singing softly, echoes of time.

As dawn breaks over fields so wide,
We listen close, without a guide.
In every rustle, every sigh,
Echoes whisper, never die.

Timeless Dances of Souls

In shadows cast by moonlit glow,
Two hearts entwined in ebb and flow.
With every step, a story spun,
As time dissolves, they become one.

A silent rhythm, pulse of grace,
Echoes linger, in warm embrace.
Eyes like stars, they shine so bright,
Whispers dance in the velvet night.

The world may fade, but they endure,
In every glance, a love so pure.
With weary feet, they glide along,
In timeless waltz, they find their song.

A tapestry of laughter rings,
In every pause, a heart that sings.
Through ages past, and futures near,
Their souls entwined, no hint of fear.

Beneath the sky, painted in fire,
Fleeting moments they conspire.
Together caught in this sweet trance,
In the timeless, they find their dance.

In the Web of Whispers

Underneath the ancient trees,
A secret shared within the breeze.
Soft murmurs float from lips to ear,
In the web of whispers, we draw near.

Leaves rustle tales of days gone by,
Sunlight filters through the sky.
Each word a thread, connecting hearts,
A gentle bond that never parts.

With every sigh, the world slows down,
In hushed tones, the heart can drown.
Like ribbons weaving through the air,
In this web, our souls lay bare.

Time stands still, the world turns gray,
With whispered dreams, we drift away.
In the hush, we find our place,
In the web of whispers, we embrace.

Through every shadow, light will gleam,
In quiet corners, we can dream.
Together we create a sphere,
Filled with love and whispered cheer.

Streams of Silent Understanding

In quiet moments, glances pass,
Like flowing streams, our thoughts amass.
No need for words, the silence speaks,
In gentle waves, our heartache leaks.

A knowing smile, a softened sigh,
In the space between, we learn to fly.
Connections deepen, unspoken truth,
In tranquil waters, we find our youth.

Beneath the surface, currents churn,
With every touch, we live and learn.
Through empathetic eyes we find,
The solace in our hearts entwined.

Ripples dance on the pond's face,
In harmony, we find our place.
Together in this quiet flow,
Streams of understanding start to glow.

With every blink, a memory flows,
In silence shared, affection grows.
In this embrace, we learn to stand,
Flowing freely, hand in hand.

Fractal Patterns of Togetherness

In the fabric of the night we weave,
Fractal patterns, we believe.
Each moment echoes, twists and turns,
In the dance of life, our spirit yearns.

Like nature's art, we find our form,
Connections spark in any storm.
Layers build, entwined and true,
A masterpiece, created by me and you.

Each heartbeat a reflection bright,
In the chaos, we find our light.
All pieces fit, in wondrous play,
Fractal patterns guide our way.

Around the world, our colors blend,
A tapestry that will not end.
In unity, our strengths combine,
Creating art, so divine.

Through every layer, love will grow,
In the fractal's heart, we glow.
Together now, forever free,
In patterns vast, we are meant to be.

Currents of Kinship

In the river of time we flow,
Bound by the tides above and below.
Each drop a memory, sweet and clear,
Echoes of laughter, whispers we hear.

Connected by roots beneath the ground,
In the soil of love, our hearts are found.
Branches entwined, reaching for the sky,
Together we rise, never asking why.

Through storms and calm, we navigate,
A web of stories that loves create.
With every ripple, our spirits blend,
In the currents of kinship, we transcend.

We gather like stars in the night,
Shining together, a wondrous sight.
In shadows and light, we stand as one,
A journey of kinship has just begun.

Together we dance in the gentle breeze,
Embracing the moments that life affords.
In currents of kinship, forever we'll float,
A tapestry woven of love's softest coat.

Fragments of Shared Dreams

In the canvas of night, dreams take flight,
Whispers of hope, soft and bright.
Each fragment a story, waiting to be told,
A treasure of wishes, a vision to hold.

We walk through the shadows, hand in hand,
Finding our way in a promised land.
In fragments of dreams, we stitch a new fate,
Bound by the visions we cultivate.

With colors of laughter, shades of our fears,
We paint the horizon with joyful tears.
Each brush stroke a moment, a bond we weave,
In shared dreams we find the strength to believe.

Through storms that may come, we weather them true,
Crafting a tale that belongs to me and you.
In fragments we gather, a rich tapestry,
Shared dreams of our hearts will always be free.

Together we rise with the dawning light,
Chasing the shadows, embracing the bright.
In the fragments of dreams, we'll always find,
A song of our journeys, forever entwined.

Tidal Waves of Understanding

In the ocean of thoughts that gently sway,
Tidal waves come to carry us each day.
With every surge, a lesson to learn,
In the depth of our hearts, a fire will burn.

Understanding flows like water's embrace,
Guiding our steps in this quiet space.
Through highs and lows, we'll find our way,
In the waves of connection, come what may.

We dive deep into thoughts, currents collide,
Rising on waves where our truths can reside.
With every crest, we negotiate,
Tidal waves teach us to contemplate.

In the ebb and flow, we discover grace,
A dance of the heart in this sacred place.
Riding the waters of wisdom's shore,
Tidal waves whisper, "Together, explore."

In unity's embrace, we'll navigate,
Finding the calm when life is irate.
Through tidal waves of understanding we steer,
A bond that is strong, ever sincere.

Ties of the Heart

In the quiet moments, we find our way,
Ties of the heart in a soft bouquet.
Each petal a promise, each stem a vow,
Together we're anchored, here and now.

A thread of connection, invisible yet strong,
Guiding us gently, where we belong.
In laughter and tears, we weave our tale,
With ties of the heart, we will not fail.

In storms of doubt, we stand side by side,
With courage and love, our souls collide.
Through struggles and triumphs, hand in hand,
In the heart's gentle ties, we firmly stand.

Each moment we share, a spark ignites,
Lighting the dark with our shared sights.
With ties of the heart, we'll never depart,
A bond unbroken, a work of art.

In the tapestry woven, our stories unfold,
Threads of affection, pure and bold.
With ties of the heart, forever we'll be,
In love's gentle dance, eternally free.

Deep Roots in Shared Ground

In the soil where we stand,
Together we bloom and grow,
Holding on through the storms,
Our strength will always show.

Beneath the surface we weave,
A tapestry rich and wide,
Connected by dreams we share,
In this journey, side by side.

Time may test our resolve,
Yet deep roots will remain,
Entwined in love and trust,
We weather every strain.

Through whispered winds of change,
We'll face what lies ahead,
With every step we take,
Our hearts will be our thread.

As seasons come and go,
We carry memories near,
In the embrace of the earth,
Our bond will persevere.

Embraces Across the Abyss

In shadows where silence reigns,
We reach across the divide,
With open arms and hearts,
Together we will bide.

Despite the distance stark,
A light within us glows,
Binding souls through the dark,
A warmth that always knows.

The chasm feels so wide,
Yet we bravely try,
With every gentle gesture,
Our spirits learn to fly.

Through laughter and through tears,
We craft a bridge so strong,
With every shared connection,
Our hearts begin to song.

And when the storms arrive,
We'll hold each other tight,
In the beauty of our bond,
We'll find our way to light.

The Symphony of Together

In harmony we stand,
Each note a vibrant hue,
Composing our own song,
With melodies so true.

A chorus of our hearts,
Resounding near and far,
In this grand symphony,
We shine just like a star.

With kindness as the strings,
We strum through highs and lows,
Creating waves of joy,
In the way our love flows.

All voices blend as one,
A rhythm we can share,
In the dance of life's grace,
With passion in the air.

Together we compose,
A timeless, sweet refrain,
In this symphony of life,
Our bond will ever reign.

Bridges Built on Trust

Strong beams of hope and faith,
We forge a way so bright,
With every step we take,
We gaze towards the light.

Through valleys deep and wide,
We'll span the chasms long,
With every handshake shared,
Our bond grows even strong.

Trust is the plank we lay,
With care we heartily shape,
Every promise spoken,
In this journey, no escape.

Through storms that may arise,
We'll hold the lines so true,
Together we will stand,
With every trust we brew.

Our bridges will endure,
Uniting land and skies,
In this world we traverse,
Our connection never dies.

Radiant Echoes of Belonging

In the quiet hum of night,
Whispers dance in the pale light.
Hearts unite with subtle grace,
Finding warmth in this shared space.

A tapestry of dreams we weave,
In every story, we believe.
Threads of laughter, threads of tears,
Binding us across the years.

In moments sweet, in silence deep,
Promises made, awake from sleep.
Together through the storm we sail,
On the winds of love, we prevail.

In the gardens of hope we bloom,
Chasing shadows away from gloom.
Radiant echoes fill the air,
Each heartbeat sings, we are aware.

For here we find our sacred place,
In every look, a warm embrace.
Together in this life we sing,
In radiant echoes, belonging brings.

Reflections in the Waters of Affinity

Upon the lake, the stars alight,
Whispers shared in soft twilight.
Ripples dapple the surface fair,
With every glance, a tender stare.

Deep within these mirrored flows,
The light of friendship gently glows.
In currents soft, our spirits blend,
In waters deep, hearts never end.

Reflecting dreams and secret hopes,
With every wave, love deftly ropes.
The tranquil depths, a solace found,
In rippling whispers, we are bound.

Among the reeds, our stories flow,
A bond so strong, we reap and sow.
Embracing tides that ebb and swell,
In vibrant hues, we weave our spell.

Together, side by side we stand,
With open hearts, we join our hand.
In the waters, we swim along,
Reflections of affinity, our song.

Soulmates in Parallel Universes

In galaxies far, we collide,
Bound by love, an endless ride.
Through pages turned in realms unknown,
Our hearts, like stars, have brightly shone.

In every life, a spark remains,
Through different paths, we break the chains.
Parallel dreams, unbroken thread,
In invisible ties, we are led.

Time unfurls like sails in breeze,
Each moment shared brings us to ease.
Across the cosmos, our hearts sing,
In every realm, love is the king.

With stardust eyes, we seek and find,
In this vast space, our bodies twined.
Soulmates wandering, side by side,
In every universe, love's our guide.

Eternity's dance, a wondrous sight,
With every heartbeat, we take flight.
In every world, our love stays true,
Soulmates bound in a cosmic hue.

Intersections of Thought and Time

In the quiet moments we exchange,
Ideas flourish, thoughts arrange.
Where paths converge, connection grows,
Like gentle rivers, time bestows.

Each word a bridge, each glance a key,
Unlocking doors to what could be.
In conversations deep and wide,
We navigate the shifting tide.

Marks of wisdom held so dear,
In laughter shared, no place for fear.
We journey forth, hand in hand,
Across the realms of thought, we stand.

Lines of time become a thread,
We weave our visions, gently spread.
In every heartbeat, pulses rhyme,
Intersections of thought and time.

For in this space, we leave our mark,
Sparking light within the dark.
Together we explore and climb,
In the dance of thought, through endless time.

The Weave of Life

In the loom of dawn, threads glow,
Colors blend in a graceful flow.
Each moment stitches a tale anew,
Woven tight with dreams we pursue.

Twisting paths in a vibrant dance,
Interwoven fates, a sacred chance.
Every heartbeat, a knot that binds,
Stories created, love unwinds.

Beneath the stars, our patterns trace,
In evening whispers, we find our place.
Life's tapestry, a dance so grand,
Guided softly by fate's own hand.

We share the fibers, rich and rare,
A fabric of hope, spun with care.
Through storms and sun, it's sewn so tight,
A masterpiece in day and night.

In the weave of time, we each have part,
A fabric stitched from the heart.
Together we stand, bridges unbound,
In the loom of life, our joy is found.

Threads of Harmony

In the quiet morn, sweet notes arise,
Threads of harmony beneath the skies.
Melodies weave through the gentle air,
Binding us close with love and care.

Every voice a strand in the tune,
Layered softly like the light of the moon.
Together we sing in a vibrant blend,
A chorus of hearts that never end.

In the weaving dusk, our voices soar,
Echoing softly, forevermore.
Notes intertwine, a radiant light,
Filling the world with pure delight.

Threads of laughter, threads of pain,
In harmony, we learn to gain.
Each note a journey, a step we take,
In this dance of life, bonds we make.

As stars emerge, we find our pace,
Holding each other in time and space.
With every heartbeat, together we grow,
Threads of harmony in life's sweet flow.

Fingers of Fate

Silent whispers in the night,
Fingers of fate guiding our flight.
Twisting paths we do not see,
But every turn, it sets us free.

In gentle strokes, the story's penned,
With every choice, we've got a friend.
A tapestry formed by hands unseen,
Fingers of fate where we've all been.

Moments unfold in the softest glow,
Guiding us gently where we must go.
An unseen force, a gentle guide,
In the shadows where dreams abide.

Threads of destiny weaves so tight,
In the fabric of day and night.
With every heartbeat, we dance and sway,
Fingers of fate lead the way.

In the quiet hours, dreams take flight,
Fate's gentle fingers hold on tight.
With each new dawn, a path anew,
Fingers of fate, always true.

Threads of Time

In the river of time, threads flow fast,
Moments captured, shadows cast.
Each second woven in golden rays,
A tapestry of life, in myriad ways.

Seasons shift, in cycles they turn,
Threads of memories, lessons we learn.
In the fabric of years, we find our ground,
Echoes of laughter, love profound.

Time, a loom, spinning dreams so fine,
In its embrace, our spirits entwine.
Each thread a story, a life to share,
In the vast expanse, we show we care.

With every tick, threads intertwine,
Past and present, in grand design.
Where moments merge, futures align,
In the dance of life, like stars that shine.

Threads of time, we weave and bend,
In the fabric of fate, we do not end.
We are but shadows in a fleeting climb,
Together we sing the song of time.

Veils of Understanding

In the silence of thought, we wander,
Through shadows whispering soft beliefs.
Each heart a prism, light to ponder,
Unraveling truths like autumn leaves.

Glimmers of wisdom in every sigh,
We dance through questions, unsure yet wise.
With every tear, a new world draws nigh,
Fostering bridges where knowledge lies.

The layers we wear, both fragile and strong,
Conceal the colors of our hidden dreams.
Together we weave a beautiful song,
In harmony, nothing is as it seems.

With open minds, we learn and embrace,
What binds us together, a shared grace.
In understanding's light, we find our place,
Finding solace in the human race.

So let us lift the veils we create,
Explore the depths of love, shed our fate.
Through every heartbeat, we contemplate,
For it is in unity we cultivate.

Chords Strummed on Destiny's Harp

In twilight's glow, notes softly play,
Life's melody danced under the stars.
With every string, we find our way,
Chasing echoes that resound from afar.

Moments collide like a fervent tune,
Fate whispers secrets through silken air.
Each heartbeat synchronizes with the moon,
Painting dreams, weaving hopes with care.

Echoes of laughter, a harmonious blend,
Unseen connections, binding all hearts.
With every challenge, we learn to mend,
Finding strength in the silent parts.

To strum the chords of passion anew,
We pluck the heartstrings of dreams untold.
In destiny's dance, we find what is true,
With every note, the future unfolds.

In the symphony of existence, we sway,
Together we play, unfurling each day.
Strummed by the hands of life's grand ballet,
Creating a rhythm that will not decay.

Portraits of Shared Existence

In still frames, lives intertwine,
Captured moments speaking in hues.
Against the canvas, souls align,
Creating a masterpiece from their dues.

With every brushstroke, stories unfold,
Of love and laughter, sorrow and strife.
A gallery of memories, bold,
Each portrait reflects the dance of life.

Eyes that glimmer with untold tales,
Whispers of hope in every gaze.
Shared experiences, like gentle gales,
Flowing together in autumn's haze.

The colors of struggle blend with the bright,
A mosaic of hearts, forever entwined.
In shadows and light, we find our fight,
Each life a masterpiece, uniquely designed.

So let us celebrate this vibrant art,
In every portrait, examine the heart.
For in shared existence, we each play a part,
Creating a world where love can impart.

Threads that Bind

In the weave of life, threads entwine,
Each fiber carrying a silent vow.
We stitch our dreams in patterns divine,
Finding strength in the here and now.

A tapestry of souls, rich and bright,
Interwoven in joys and in pain.
In every corner, love ignites,
Uniting us through sunshine and rain.

The golden strands of kinship bind,
In the fabric of time, we find our grace.
Together we journey, heart intertwined,
Building a home in this sacred space.

As seasons change, the threads may fray,
Yet still we hold the tapestry near.
In every stitch, memories stay,
A reminder of love that conquers fear.

So let us cherish this woven design,
In the threads that bind, we shall shine.
For in every life, our destinies align,
Creating a masterpiece, uniquely divine.

Winds that Part

In the hush of dawn, the winds take flight,
Carrying whispers of hopes anew.
They dance through valleys, kissing the night,
Painting dreams with every gentle hue.

Though paths may diverge, the heart knows well,
In the echo of breezes, love remains.
Stories of journeys, within us swell,
As we wander through joys and pains.

The currents may shift, yet we hold tight,
To memories woven in time and trust.
Through every storm, we seek the light,
In the power of love, we believe, we must.

With every gust, we learn to let go,
Embracing the change that life brings near.
For in each departure, the seeds we sow,
Are blossoms of friendship, forever clear.

So let us honor the winds that part,
For change is a canvas, a brand-new start.
In every farewell, a promise shall chart,
The horizon of dreams, woven in the heart.

Dances of Distant Stars

In the dark they sway and spin,
Twinkling lights where dreams begin.
Galaxies weave through the night,
With a grace that feels so right.

Cosmic rhythms play a tune,
Echoing in the silver moon.
Whispers of time twist and glide,
In the vastness, love can't hide.

Each spark tells a tale so deep,
Of wishes made and secrets to keep.
Beyond reach but never far,
We find solace in each star.

They dance on waves of dark and light,
Guiding souls through endless flight.
In this silence, hearts can see,
The beauty of our mystery.

Together in the night we stand,
Feeling threads of fate so grand.
In the cosmos, we belong,
United in a timeless song.

Whispered Bonds in Shadows

In the twilight's gentle hush,
A bond forms in silent rush.
Fingers reach through the unknown,
In shadows, soft love is grown.

Shared glances spark unspoken tales,
In every twist, affection prevails.
Beneath the moon's tender gaze,
Hearts connect in quiet ways.

Like whispers lost in the breeze,
Each moment, we aim to seize.
In the dark, no fear to show,
These ties bind us heart to soul.

Stars bear witness to our plight,
As we brave the depths of night.
Through shadows, our spirits soar,
Finding strength in the encore.

In the whispers, we abide,
With love, we take the tide.
Together through the fading light,
Shadows dance, we hold on tight.

Lifelines of Unseen Ties

In the fabric of daily life,
Invisible threads weave through strife.
With each heartbeat, ties connect,
Binding souls that time respects.

With laughter shared and tears released,
Our bonds grow strong, fears are ceased.
Through distance vast, we still can feel,
A lifeline formed, forever real.

In moments brief yet truly bright,
Voices echo through the night.
Uniting us beyond the place,
Each heartbeat, a warm embrace.

Through the storms and sunny days,
These connections never sway.
Anchored deep in the core of we,
With unseen ties, we are free.

A tapestry spun from desire,
We lift each other higher.
In every laugh and tear we find,
Lifelines forged, forever entwined.

Waves of Shared Existence

On the shore, the waves will rise,
Carrying dreams beneath the skies.
Each crest and trough, a story true,
Echoes of me, of you, of us too.

In the rhythm of ocean's breath,
We dance together, life and death.
The currents pull, the tides will shift,
In their embrace, our spirits lift.

Through the calm and tempest's roar,
We embrace what lies in store.
Together, we weather the sea,
Bound by waves of destiny.

Moments shared, we break the mold,
In every drop, our tales unfold.
With laughter, love, and silent cries,
In the waves, our truth lies.

In the ebb and flow we find,
Connections deep, forever kind.
Together, in this dance divine,
Waves of life, your hand in mine.

Threads of Laughter and Tears

In laughter, joy wraps its arms tight,
A dance of memories, day and night.
Yet tears may fall like gentle rain,
Each drop a story, a trace of pain.

We weave our tales with golden thread,
In colors bright, in shadows spread.
Each moment shared, a timeless stitch,
Our hearts entwined, a perfect pitch.

Through ups and downs, we find our way,
With every laugh, we chase the gray.
In laughter's echo, tears dissolve,
Together we grow, together we evolve.

A tapestry rich, life's canvas grand,
With every fiber, we take a stand.
In joy and sorrow, we are one,
In threads of laughter, life weighs a ton.

So hand in hand, we bravely tread,
With love that shines, and tears that shed.
For in the weave of our shared fate,
A masterpiece blooms, never too late.

Hidden Roads of Familiarity

Down hidden paths, where shadows glide,
We wander forth, side by side.
Each step we take, a story grows,
In whispered tales the heart knows.

Familiar corners, faces glow,
In places where the soft winds blow.
With laughter shared, our spirits rise,
In secret spaces, no disguise.

We trace the lines of time's embrace,
Finding solace, a warm place.
In quiet moments, we pause and breathe,
In the threads of life, we weave and seethe.

Through hidden roads where shadows dance,
We catch a glimpse, a fleeting chance.
Each twist and turn brings us near,
In the calm, we conquer fear.

Together we stroll, our journey we share,
In the comfort of knowing you're always there.
In the maze of life, we roam free,
In hidden roads, just you and me.

The Pulse of Shared Dreams

In twilight's glow, our dreams ignite,
A symphony of hopes, taking flight.
With every heartbeat, we align,
A rhythm of trust, pure and divine.

Through shadows dark, we find the light,
In visions shared, we hold on tight.
With whispered wishes, we carve our way,
In the pulse of dreams, we choose to stay.

Together we build, with hands entwined,
A world of wonders, beautifully designed.
With hearts open wide, we brave the storm,
In every trial, our spirits warm.

Each fleeting moment, a treasure we hold,
A story unfolding, in colors so bold.
With laughter and love, our voices soar,
In the pulse of dreams, we yearn for more.

So let us dance to this beat divine,
In harmony found, together we shine.
For in the tapestry of this shared theme,
Our souls intertwine, living the dream.

Bonded by the Same Sky

Beneath the stars, where dreams reside,
We find our bond, a cosmic tide.
In the depths of night, together we gaze,
Chasing dreams in the moon's soft haze.

Each twinkling light, a story it tells,
Of laughter and tears, of casting spells.
In the vastness of space, we find our way,
For love and hope nobly sway.

Through storms we weather, hand in hand,
With hearts united, we take a stand.
In the sunlit morning, our spirits rise,
Forever bonded under the same skies.

The clouds may gather, the winds may churn,
Yet in our hearts, the fires burn.
For every sunset paints our truth,
In hues of love, in vibrant youth.

Together we dream, together we strive,
In the expanse where our spirits thrive.
With stars above, we always know,
We're bonded forever, wherever we go.

Threads of Unseen Bonds

In shadows soft, we weave our dreams,
With whispers light, like flowing streams.
A tapestry of hearts entwined,
In every beat, our souls aligned.

The silent threads that bind us tight,
Are woven close, out of plain sight.
Through trials faced and laughter shared,
In every moment, love is bared.

The strength we find in quiet grace,
Connects us in this sacred space.
Invisible, yet felt so true,
These threads unite me, and you too.

Each bond a story, softly spun,
Together, we are never done.
Our lives like colors paint the sky,
In harmony, we learn to fly.

So let us cherish what we share,
In every heartbeat, every prayer.
These unseen bonds will hold us near,
A love that conquers doubt and fear.

Whispers Across Time

In echoes past, our voices blend,
Through ages lost, our hearts extend.
A gentle nudge from time unseen,
Connects us in a timeless dream.

Across the years, we send our hopes,
Like feathered dove on sunset slopes.
With every breath, the memories hum,
A symphony of what is to come.

Beneath the stars, our fates entwine,
A dance of souls that feels divine.
With every thought, a bridge we build,
In silent awe, our dreams fulfilled.

Through love's soft call, we wander far,
With guiding light, our shining star.
With threads of gold, our lives are spun,
In whispered truths, we become one.

So let us walk through echoes bright,
With open hearts and minds alight.
Together bound by time's embrace,
In every moment, find our place.

Ties That Bridge the Divide

In distant lands, where rivers flow,
Our stories mix, with truths we know.
A bridge of hope, where hearts align,
In unity, our spirits shine.

Through valleys deep and mountains high,
The ties we forge will never die.
Each journey taken, side by side,
In every step, we cast aside.

The laughter shared, the tears we shed,
Are threads of love that journey spread.
Across the worlds, we find our way,
In every dawn, a brand new day.

With open arms, we greet the chance,
To bridge the gaps in this grand dance.
In common ground, our souls ignite,
In fierce embrace, we find the light.

So let us rise beyond the pain,
And celebrate the ties we've gained.
With fearless hearts, we march ahead,
Together strong, our fears are shed.

Echoes of Unity

Upon the hills, where voices rise,
A chorus strong beneath the skies.
With every song, a bond is made,
In echoes soft, our fears do fade.

In unity, we stand as one,
Together shining, like the sun.
Through every trial, we hold the line,
In every heartbeat, love will shine.

With arms outstretched toward the light,
We gather close, igniting bright.
In every pulse, in every sigh,
An echo calls, we cannot lie.

The world may shift, but we remain,
In fierce connection, through joy and pain.
With open hearts, we pave the way,
In harmony, we find our stay.

So let us raise our voices clear,
In every note, let's cast the fear.
With echoes bold, our song will soar,
In unity, we rise once more.

Layers of Light and Shadow

In the dawn, shadows stretch wide,
Light whispers secrets, softly implied.
Colors dance, a vivid embrace,
While darkness lingers, in hidden space.

Clouds drift slowly, painting the sky,
Moments captured, time passing by.
Each hue speaks of woes and delight,
Layers of stories wrapped up tight.

The sun dips low, hues start to fade,
Shadows now lengthen, darkness invade.
Yet within the gloom, glimmers reside,
Hope's gentle flicker, our faithful guide.

Night unveils mysteries, soft and deep,
In silence, dreams wander, and seep.
Stars tremble softly in velvet vast,
A blend of present, future, and past.

Embrace both sides, the light and dark,
For in their union, we find a spark.
Layers revealed, through trials we grow,
In the realm of shadows, light will flow.

Celestial Connections in Motion

Stars pulse gently in the night,
Whispers of worlds, a wondrous flight.
Veils of time, they unravel wide,
In cosmic dances, we feel their guide.

Comets blaze across the sky,
Their fleeting paths, we wonder why.
Every twinkle tells a story,
Ancient echoes of faded glory.

The moon hangs low, a guardian bright,
Waves of silence bathe us in light.
Each phase brings change, a constant theme,
Connections forged in a celestial dream.

Galaxies spiral, in infinite grace,
Time and space blend, they intertwine and embrace.
We weave our dreams with stardust threads,
Boundless journeys where the heart treads.

In swirling orbits, we find our place,
Underneath the cosmos, an endless chase.
With every glance to the heavens above,
We celebrate, through stars, our love.

Merging Paths of Fate

Two roads converge beneath the trees,
Fate's gentle whisper rides the breeze.
In the stillness, choices await,
Mapping out futures that intertwine fate.

Footsteps echo on the winding trail,
Stories entwined, we will not fail.
Moments grasped, like gold in hand,
Drawing us closer, a fate so grand.

Every glance shared, a spark ignites,
In the twilight, two souls in flight.
Hearts open wide, like petals in bloom,
Drawing together, dispelling all gloom.

The tapestry we weave unfolds bright,
Threads of laughter and love in sight.
Merging paths, no longer two,
A journey forward, just me and you.

Hand in hand through the twist and turn,
With each new dawn, for love we yearn.
Destinies woven, a story to create,
Embracing the magic of our shared fate.

Footsteps on Shared Sand

By the shore where waters kiss land,
Footprints linger, side by side they stand.
Echoes of laughter mix with the tide,
As sun sets low, we turn with pride.

Waves roll gently, secrets they share,
Each grain of sand tells tales laid bare.
Moments captured in soft golden light,
A promise eternal in the fading night.

Seagulls cry out, calling us near,
In the salty air, love's whispers clear.
Together we walk, with hearts in sync,
Sharing our dreams with each gentle wink.

The horizon beckons, painted in hues,
Every new day brings fresh views.
Together we build, a castle of dreams,
Where love flows freely like flowing streams.

As tides may shift and sands may change,
Our bond remains strong, never estranged.
Through storms and sunshine, hand in hand,
We leave our mark on this shared sand.

Tethered to the Same Stars

In night's embrace we stand so close,
Tethered dreams, where silence flows.
Beneath the gaze of endless skies,
We find our truth, where darkness lies.

Stars whisper secrets of distant days,
In cosmic dances, our hearts ablaze.
A universe shared, so vast, so deep,
Awakens the wonders we dared to keep.

Guided by light, we traverse the space,
With every heartbeat, a sacred grace.
Through every shadow, we navigate,
Together we forge a celestial fate.

While time may flow like a gentle stream,
In the same skies, we dare to dream.
No distance can sever the bond we share,
For we are one in the starlit air.

And as the dawn approaches near,
We carry forth what we hold dear.
Each moment spent, a pulse in the night,
Tethered forever, hearts shining bright.

Cascading Moments of Touch

In gentle whispers, fingers meet,
A tender dance, so soft, discreet.
Each fleeting brush ignites a spark,
Cascading moments in the dark.

Like raindrops falling, a symphony,
Echoing in sweet harmony.
Every heartbeat traces a line,
A map of love, a sacred sign.

Memories linger like fragrant blooms,
In the quiet spaces of our rooms.
With every gaze, our souls collide,
In an embrace where dreams reside.

We weave our tales with silent vows,
In the tapestry of here and now.
With hands entwined, we drift away,
In cascading moments where hearts sway.

Amongst the stars, our laughter soars,
As time stands still, in open doors.
Wrapped in warmth, we find our place,
In cascading moments, love's embrace.

Harmonies of Heartbeats

In the quiet hum of gentle night,
Heartbeats echo, soft and light.
A rhythm shared, a living song,
In this space, we both belong.

With every pulse, the world fades away,
In harmonies, we choose to stay.
Our whispers blend like colors bright,
A canvas painted in pure delight.

Together, we find a perfect tune,
Under the watch of the silver moon.
In every laugh and soft-spoken word,
A symphony grand, perfectly heard.

As time waltzes, our spirits soar,
Through melodies cherished, we both explore.
In the dance of life, we are entwined,
With harmonies of heartbeats, aligned.

In every moment, love's refrain,
We recognize joy, we embrace the pain.
With open hearts, we bravely strive,
In the music of us, we come alive.

Luminous Conversations Beyond Words

In twilight's glow, we share our thoughts,
With silent glances, connection sought.
Unspoken dreams in the softest night,
Luminous conversations take flight.

Words may falter, but hearts declare,
A language woven in the air.
Through every smile, an echo heard,
In the stillness, the world is blurred.

With tender gestures, we weave our tales,
In the spaces where love prevails.
Beyond the chatter, our souls converse,
In the gentle beauty of the universe.

Time stands still in this sacred place,
In luminous moments, we find our grace.
The light within us, a radiant spark,
Illuminates shadows, banishing dark.

In the dance of life, we are entwined,
Exploring depths of the unseen kind.
Together we flourish, in silence, we soar,
Luminous conversations forevermore.

Blossoms of Brotherhood

In the garden where we stand,
Our hands entwined, a gentle band.
With laughter echoed all around,
In every heart, our love is found.

We share the warmth of sunlight's grace,
With every smile, the world we trace.
Together we can face the night,
In unity, we find our light.

Through storms and trials, we will grow,
Like blossoms in the morning glow.
In every challenge that we meet,
Our bond makes every moment sweet.

From whispered dreams in shadows cast,
To soaring hopes that hold us fast.
In brotherhood, we rise anew,
As petals soft kissed by the dew.

When roots entwine beneath the earth,
They nurture dreams, give them birth.
In every struggle, hand in hand,
We find the strength to understand.

Seasons of Togetherness

Spring brings whispers on the breeze,
As flowers bloom beneath the trees.
We laugh and dance beneath the sun,
In every moment, two as one.

Summer's warmth invites the joy,
As children play with every toy.
In golden fields, we chase the days,
Our hearts aglow in sun's warm rays.

Autumn's leaves, a canvas bright,
We gather close, a cozy night.
With cider warm and stories shared,
In every heart, our love declared.

Winter blankets all in white,
With frosty air, the world feels right.
Together by the fire's glow,
In seasons' change, our spirits grow.

Through every season, hand in hand,
We find our place, we understand.
In laughter, love, and memories,
Together always, as we please.

Interlaced Journeys

Two paths converging in the wood,
Where whispers tell what's understood.
With every step, we forge our fate,
In journeys shared, we resonate.

From mountain heights to valley low,
Together we embrace the flow.
Through winding roads, both rough and smooth,
In every challenge, we will move.

With compass hearts, we'll find our way,
In unity, we greet each day.
From dusk till dawn, our spirits soar,
In every stride, we seek for more.

As rivers meld and oceans meet,
Our shared adventures feel complete.
In tales of wonder, side by side,
We share the dreams that burn inside.

These interlaced journeys, so divine,
With you beside me, all will shine.
Through every chapter, hand in hand,
Together always, we will stand.

Signs in the Stratosphere

In starlit skies, we seek the signs,
Constellations drawing sacred lines.
With wonder in our gazing eyes,
We chase the dreams that fill the skies.

Like comets blazing through the night,
Our hopes take flight, a dazzling sight.
With every twinkle, sparks ignite,
In harmony, we find our light.

Clouds may gather and shadows fall,
Yet love remains, a steadfast call.
In every storm, we stand as one,
Our hearts united, we have won.

With every dawn, a fresh new chance,
Beneath the sun, we weave our dance.
In skies above, our spirits soar,
In unity, we seek for more.

So let us write upon the stars,
Our story told, no matter how far.
In the vastness of this endless sphere,
Together always, year by year.

Chasing Shadows

In the twilight, whispers creep,
Ghostly forms begin to leap.
Every corner holds a mask,
Secrets hide in dusk's soft flask.

Fading echoes of the past,
Moments gone, forever cast.
With each step, the shadows dance,
Inviting dreams to take a chance.

Fleeting glimpses fade away,
Lost in night, we long to stay.
Chasing forms that slip between,
Fingers grasping what once seemed.

A flicker haunts the lover's sigh,
In the dark, our aims comply.
Together we can face our fears,
But the shadows draw us near.

Always seeking, never found,
Life's maze, it twirls around.
In these folds, our souls entwine,
Chasing shadows, yours and mine.

Merging Light

Two horizons blend as one,
The dawn breaks where we begun.
Colors dance in soft embrace,
Creating joy in every space.

Radiant rays through forest trees,
Nature hums with gentle breeze.
Warmth surrounds, a sweet caress,
In this moment, we are blessed.

Footsteps echo on the shore,
Waves whisper promises and more.
Together we will forge our way,
Merging light, come what may.

Every heartbeat draws us near,
In our eyes, there's no more fear.
Through the storm and through the night,
We will shine, a brilliant light.

Paths unfold beneath our feet,
In the twilight, life feels sweet.
Each soft glow a guiding spark,
Merging light dispels the dark.

Knots of Familiarity

Threads we weave, time's gentle art,
Knots of familiarity, from the start.
In laughter shared and quiet sighs,
Binding hearts, where comfort lies.

Stories told beneath the stars,
In every moment, love's memoirs.
Memories wrapped in tender ties,
Binding us, no need for 'why'.

In every twist, a journey paved,
Through storms weathered, dreams engraved.
Holding close what time bestows,
In our hearts, true love still grows.

With every tear and every cheer,
Knots of love draw us near.
Familiar paths where we belong,
In this bond, forever strong.

Together we shall face the tide,
With every knot, hope as our guide.
Embracing life, both joy and pain,
Knots of familiarity remain.

Resilient Ties of Heartstrings

In the silence, love's refrain,
Resilient ties won't break in vain.
With strength woven through their core,
Heartstrings pull, forevermore.

Through trials faced and laughter shared,
In every moment, we have dared.
Bound by loyalty, warmth, and grace,
In the depths, our hopes embrace.

Each thread tells tales of what we've found,
Stories binding us, profound.
Carrying dreams that intertwine,
Resilient chords, so pure, divine.

In the storm, when spirits sway,
These heartstrings lead us on our way.
With every challenge, we will thrive,
Resilient ties keep love alive.

Hand in hand, as seasons change,
Through ups and downs, we rearrange.
Together, forever, we'll redeem,
Resilient ties—the strongest seam.

Crystals of Connection

In fragile light, reflections play,
Crystals shine, in bright array.
Each facet holds a glimpse of truth,
Anchoring dreams of love and youth.

Glimmers of hope in every soul,
Connected hearts that make us whole.
Through the chaos, we shall find,
Crystals of connection, intertwined.

In the silence, echoes gleam,
Promises wrapped in every dream.
Pulsing light that guides our way,
Crystals brightening each new day.

Through the shadows and the shine,
In every moment, your heart is mine.
Together, we'll forge a master key,
Unlocking love with purity.

With every challenge, we will rise,
These crystals bridge the vastest skies.
In unity, our spirits dance,
Crystals of connection, our sweet chance.

Reflections of Reunion

In the twilight glow, we gather near,
Echoes of laughter ringing clear.
Memories woven, stories unfold,
Hearts intertwined, a warmth to behold.

Time may pass, but bonds remain,
Through joy and sorrow, through loss and gain.
In the mirror of love, we see our grace,
A tapestry rich, no time can erase.

With open arms and eyes so bright,
Each moment cherished, pure delight.
We walk together, no longer alone,
In the garden of friendship, our seeds are sown.

The sunset paints the sky in gold,
A promise of stories yet to be told.
With every heartbeat, the ties grow strong,
Together we rise, where we all belong.

As shadows dance in fading light,
We hold each other, hearts ignite.
In this reunion, love's sweet embrace,
A reflection of joy, a sacred space.

Open Doors to Tomorrow

Each dawn brings hope, a chance anew,
With open doors, the world in view.
Steps of courage on paths unknown,
A journey awaits, seeds to be sown.

Together we dream, visions unfold,
With faith in our hearts, and dreams to be bold.
The future's a canvas, colors we choose,
With each stroke of wisdom, we cannot lose.

In the light of reason, shadows dispel,
Voices united, we all can tell.
With hands intertwined, we rise and strive,
In unity's strength, our spirits thrive.

Open doors beckon, horizons expand,
With love as our guide, we take a stand.
In the realm of tomorrow, possibilities gleam,
Together we'll weave the fabric of dream.

With laughter as fuel, and kindness our key,
We turn the locks, set our spirits free.
In the journey of life, we play our part,
Open doors to tomorrow, led by the heart.

Shadows of Solidarity

In shadows we gather, voices align,
Through struggles faced, our spirits shine.
Together we stand, united we fight,
In this shared journey, we find our light.

Hands stretched forth, in strength we trust,
Through laughter and tears, we rise from dust.
In the depths of night, we find our way,
Guided by hope, to a brighter day.

With open hearts, we share the load,
In resilience forged, our paths bestowed.
We lift each other, when spirits are low,
In the shadows of solidarity, love will grow.

The silent whispers of pain we mend,
In this alliance, we are more than friends.
Through storms we weather, hand in hand,
In the tapestry of life, together we stand.

Through the trials faced, we weave our song,
In the fabric of unity, we all belong.
With every heartbeat, a promise we make,
In shadows of solidarity, no one shall break.

A Symphony of Togetherness

In the orchestra of life, we play our part,
Notes of compassion, a song from the heart.
Each voice distinct in harmony's embrace,
Creating a symphony, a beautiful space.

Through laughter and tears, we compose our score,
In moments shared, love's music we pour.
With every heartbeat, a rhythm enriches,
In this dance of life, passion bewitches.

With strings of support, and brass of cheer,
We navigate through both joy and fear.
In unity's chorus, our spirits take flight,
Filling the silence with colors of light.

Together we rise, like waves on the shore,
In the concert of souls, we crave for more.
With drumbeats of courage, we march with pride,
In the symphony of togetherness, side by side.

The finale approaches, yet we stand tall,
In the beauty we crafted, we've given our all.
With echoes of laughter, and love that won't cease,
In this grand orchestra, we've found our peace.

Mosaic Whispers of Kinship

In shadows cast by evening's light,
Voices blend in gentle flight.
Threads of laughter, stories weave,
In each heart, a space to grieve.

Colors bright, though sometimes gray,
Unity in every fray.
Together we rise, side by side,
In this dance, our souls collide.

Ancient bonds that time can't sever,
Whispers soft, a bond forever.
Mosaic hearts, both wild and free,
In love's embrace, we dare to be.

With every step, a tale unfolds,
In tender hands, the truth beholds.
Seasons change, yet here we stand,
Crafted life, a guiding hand.

Together woven, linked in fate,
In every joy, we resonate.
Through trials faced, our strength combined,
A tapestry of hearts aligned.

The Fabric of Existence

In threads of time, we find our way,
Stitches bind the dark and day.
Each moment a wisp, a thread so fine,
Woven dreams on paths that intertwine.

In vibrant hues, the fabric breathes,
A tapestry of hopes and heaves.
We dance beneath the stars' soft glow,
Life's vibrant journey, ebb and flow.

Winds of change, they sweep and soar,
Through open doors, we seek for more.
The loom of life, both kind and cruel,
We gather wisdom, our greatest jewel.

Fragile threads may sometimes fray,
Yet beauty shines in a unique way.
In every tear, a lesson learned,
In every pause, our souls have yearned.

We weave our stories, hand in hand,
Across the vast, uncharted land.
With every stitch, we form the whole,
A fabric rich with heart and soul.

Woven Journeys of Spirit

Across the mountains, rivers wide,
In every heart, a song to bide.
Our spirits soar on winds of grace,
In every journey, we find our place.

Threads of longing, paths unseen,
In every corner, love's routine.
With every heartbeat, closer drawn,
In whispered prayers, we greet the dawn.

Through valleys deep and skies so vast,
Our souls are linked, forever cast.
In laughter's echo, pain's release,
We stitch our journeys, finding peace.

In distant lands, familiar faces,
Through life's journeys, sacred spaces.
With every touch, a spark ignites,
In shared moments, we claim the nights.

Woven with dreams, the universe,
In every heartbeat, a whispered verse.
As spirits dance in cosmic flow,
We find our kinship, ever grow.

Ripples of Resounding Love

In tranquil waters, ripples spread,
Each drop a promise softly said.
Building bridges with gentle hands,
Love resounds in distant lands.

In every heartbeat, waves do rise,
Caressing shores beneath the skies.
With open hearts, we start to sing,
In harmony, our spirits cling.

Through storms that shake and winds that roar,
Love's essence binds us evermore.
In quiet moments, tender and meek,
In every glance, the words we speak.

Like whispers shared in twilight's glow,
The seeds of kindness, gently sow.
In every challenge that we share,
Ripples of love, beyond compare.

Together we rise, a tidal wave,
In love's embrace, we find the brave.
With every rise and every fall,
The echo of our hearts, a call.

Matchsticks in the Cosmic Dance

In the dark, they flicker bright,
Small sparks of fading light.
Fingers brush 'gainst the night,
Creating warmth, pure delight.

In cosmic whirl, they sway,
Igniting dreams on display.
In stillness, they play,
Painting shadows that stay.

From hidden depths, they rise,
Flashes of ancient skies.
In moments, they disguise,
Whispers of life's surprise.

When trembling hands unite,
They dance with pure insight.
Against the vast, endless sight,
A flame ignites the night.

Each matchstick's fragile grace,
Holding time in its place.
In the cosmos, we trace,
A journey we embrace.

Glimmers of Kindred Spirits

In a crowded room, they meet,
Silent smiles, hearts discreet.
With every glance, they greet,
A rhythm soft and sweet.

Kindred souls, a gentle glow,
Echoes of tales we know.
Through laughter, love will flow,
In this bond, we grow.

Two hearts beating as one,
Underneath the setting sun.
In moments swiftly spun,
A thread that can't be undone.

Through storms and joy, we sail,
In the winds, a shared trail.
Together, we set the scale,
In whispers that won't pale.

With each memory, we weave,
A tapestry we believe.
In love, we shall conceive,
A strength that won't deceive.

Tapestries of Unseen Hands

In shadows where dreams weave,
Threads of fate gently cleave.
Hands unseen yet they leave,
Marks of joy, webs we weave.

In quiet corners, they work,
Stitching smiles, with a smirk.
Creating light from the murk,
Where secrets softly lurk.

Each tug pulls at the heart,
Binding souls that won't part.
With every intricate art,
A masterpiece from the start.

Colors clash and embrace,
A dance of time and space.
In patterns we find grace,
In laughter, love's warm trace.

These hands may remain unseen,
Crafting joy in between.
In the fabric, we glean,
A world that feels like a dream.

The Language of Unspoken Bonds

In silence, we share breath,
Words unspoken beyond death.
A language free from the heft,
In every glance, a depth.

Through the nights we wander close,
Each heartbeat, a silent prose.
In soft echoes, we compose,
A symphony, love's rose.

No need for words to explain,
Through the joy and through the pain.
Together we will remain,
In the sun, in the rain.

In gestures, soft as a wing,
Life's meaning starts to sing.
In connections, we find spring,
A unity so freeing.

So let the silence unfold,
A story yet to be told.
In the warmth that we hold,
An embrace, purest gold.

Dreams Intertwined in the Night

In the whisper of the stars, we soar,
Into realms where shadows dance and explore.
Hearts unite in the glow of fading light,
A tapestry woven, wrapped in the night.

Dreams like rivers, winding and free,
Carrying echoes of what we could be.
In the stillness, our hopes intertwine,
A promise held softly, forever divine.

Every sigh a flutter, every glance a spark,
As we wander together through the limitless dark.
In this space where silence blooms,
Our souls find solace, dispelling the glooms.

With each breath taken, our visions align,
Painting horizons with colors so fine.
And as the dawn brushes shadows away,
We hold these dreams close, come what may.

When daylight breaks, we'll chase the unseen,
Together we'll thrive, the spaces between.
In the magic of whispers, we remain,
Bound by the night, we dance once again.

Celestial Bearings of Belonging

Underneath the vast, unbroken sky,
Stars form patterns that never say goodbye.
In the cosmos, our hearts beat as one,
Finding our place where all dreams have begun.

Each constellation tells tales of old,
Of journeys taken, of hearts brave and bold.
In this universe, we carve our own path,
With love as our compass, igniting our wrath.

The moonlight guides us on nights so serene,
While whispers of stardust linger between.
In the dance of planets, we find our tune,
Orbiting truths that make the heart swoon.

Gravity draws us amidst cosmic sway,
Finding warmth in the chaos of day.
In this realm of wonder, we lay our claim,
Together forever, in love's sacred name.

As we navigate life's celestial sea,
With you by my side, I'm endlessly free.
In this cosmic embrace, we belong,
Sharing our light, forever strong.

The Quiet After the Storm of Us

When thunder fades into memory's embrace,
And silence cloaks our once turbulent space.
Raindrops linger like tears on the ground,
In the echo of love, peace can be found.

Skies are clear, and the world feels new,
In the stillness, I reach out for you.
Hearts mend slowly, like branches that sway,
In the breeze, where yesterday fades away.

The sun breaks forth, painting shadows long,
Reminding us gently where we both belong.
In this sacred calm, we redefine,
The space that was ours, the love that is fine.

Together we wander, hand in hand,
Through gardens where hope and healing stand.
In the quiet moments, our souls are heard,
Speaking the truth without a single word.

With every sunrise, we rise anew,
Finding strength in the bond that we knew.
In fragile beauty, our hearts stay aligned,
After the storm, love is redefined.

Seedlings in Shared Soil

In the garden where dreams softly bloom,
We plant our wishes, dispelling the gloom.
Each seedling nurtured with care and with love,
Roots intertwining like stars up above.

Together we water these fragile hopes,
With laughter and kindness, we rise and cope.
In this sacred space, our spirits will grow,
Tending the soil where our hearts overflow.

As seasons change, we learn and adapt,
In the warmth of connection, we're never trapped.
Sunshine and rain shape our tender embrace,
In this garden of fortune, we find our place.

With every blossom, stories unfold,
Of courage and dreams that are daring and bold.
In the dance of the petals, life carries on,
Together forever, our bond will be strong.

And in the harvest, we gather our joys,
In laughter and love, we become life's toys.
In the shared soil, our future's entwined,
Together, forever, with hearts aligned.

Entwined in Existence

In shadows cast, our lives align,
Two paths converge, a fate divine.
With whispered words, hearts intertwine,
In every moment, love's design.

Through trials faced, we find our way,
In laughter shared, the light of day.
Together, strong, we won't betray,
This bond that holds, come what may.

The stars above, a guiding light,
In darkest hours, we claim our right.
With every breath, we soar in flight,
Entwined in hope, our spirits bright.

Time's gentle stream flows ever on,
In memories sweet, we are reborn.
No distance can our hearts have drawn,
Through every dusk, we greet the dawn.

In quiet moments, stillness speaks,
The language of the soul it seeks.
With open hearts, each joy we peak,
Entwined in love, together we tweak.

Mosaics of Memory

Each shard of time, a story told,
In vibrant hues, both meek and bold.
Fragments of laughter, tears of gold,
In mosaics of memory, we behold.

Colorful pieces, scattered wide,
Each holds a moment, none can hide.
In whispered echoes, dreams reside,
Together, past and present glide.

A tapestry woven with care and grace,
In fleeting moments, we find our place.
Through joy and sorrow, all we embrace,
In the gallery of life, we trace.

What once was lost, now shines anew,
In every memory, shades of blue.
Together, we wander, hearts true,
In this mosaic, me and you.

The art of living, each stroke we make,
In laughter's sound, or heart's small ache.
With every heartbeat, dreams awake,
We shape our world, for love's own sake.

Dance of Destiny

With every step, the rhythms flow,
In destiny's dance, we come to know.
Together we spin, in moonlit glow,
A waltz of wonder, a sweet tableau.

With hands entwined, we take the chance,
In life's grand hall, we dare to dance.
Each twist and turn, a fleeting glance,
In passion's fire, we find romance.

The music swells, our hearts leap high,
Under the stars, we touch the sky.
With every beat, we dare to fly,
In fate's embrace, we live, not shy.

Through shifting tides, we find our beat,
In sync with time, our lives complete.
With every sway, our souls repeat,
A dance of destiny, bittersweet.

As seasons change, our rhythm lasts,
In shadows cast, the truth contrasts.
Yet through it all, our love steadfast,
In this dance of life, we'll hold it fast.

Bridges of Empathy

On gentle paths, we find our way,
Building bridges where hearts can stay.
In moments shared, we learn to play,
With open arms, come what may.

We reach across the chasms wide,
In quiet understanding, we abide.
With kindness as our trusted guide,
In bridges built, love won't divide.

Every story told, a soul laid bare,
Through trials faced, we show we care.
In laughter shared, the burdens rare,
With bridges of empathy, we dare.

In colors bright, our hearts entwine,
Each thread a promise, gently align.
With open hearts, our spirits shine,
In unity's dance, our lives combine.

Together we stand, like ancient trees,
Rooted deep in the autumn breeze.
Through storms we grow, in harmony's ease,
On bridges of empathy, love's keys.

Seasons Shifting in Union

The leaves turn gold, then fade away,
Whispers of change in the crisp, cool air.
Winter blankets all in silent gray,
Nature's rhythm, a dance so rare.

Spring blossoms forth with colors bright,
Awakening life from slumber's night.
Summer sings loud and warms the earth,
In every heart, it sparks a mirth.

Autumn's chill brings a gentle sigh,
Painting the world as it waves goodbye.
Seasons shift, yet together we stand,
In this cycle, hand in hand.

Moments of joy in sunshine and rain,
Life's tapestry, woven with pain.
Through fading days and brightening skies,
Love endures as the time flies.

Each season's song calls us apart,
Yet binds our souls, a timeless art.
In union we greet what must arrive,
Together, we learn how to thrive.

Fleeting Glances

In crowded rooms where silence speaks,
A mere moment, yet it feels so deep.
Eyes meet briefly, the language unique,
An uncharted bond we strive to keep.

A smile exchanged, a heart skips fast,
In the rush of life, time streaks by.
Yet cherish that spark, it holds us steadfast,
A fleeting glance, the purest high.

We navigate paths, both near and far,
In moments so brief, yet forever last.
Like falling stars, we are what we are,
In brief encounters, memories cast.

The world spins on, with stories untold,
Connections made in a blink of an eye.
In those passed moments, a treasure to hold,
Fleeting glances, the reason we fly.

The present fades, the past will remain,
In glances exchanged, we find our way.
Though time may rush, the warmth will sustain,
In the heart's quiet corners, they stay.

Lasting Impressions

A single word can change the day,
Like brush on canvas, strokes define.
With every laugh and every sway,
We leave our mark, intertwining lines.

In kindness shared, or hand in hand,
We weave memories through time's embrace.
A tender touch, a cherished strand,
In the heart's archives, we find our place.

Moments that linger, strong and true,
In every choice, the paths we tread.
With wisdom gained, we see anew,
Lasting impressions, our quiet thread.

In whispers soft or thunder's roar,
Life's tapestry we each contribute.
Through trials faced and open doors,
The bonds we forge, forever resolute.

As seasons change and we grow old,
In every heart, our stories thrive.
Lasting impressions, precious as gold,
In love and laughter, we are alive.

Tides of Emotions Connecting Us

Waves crash softly on the shore,
Emotions rise, then pull away.
In each heartbeat, we feel the roar,
Of longing tides that gently sway.

As friendship flows like rivers wide,
With every change, we learn to bend.
The tide we face, the joy, the pride,
A journey shared, a timeless trend.

In moments bright, the shadows swayed,
We find ourselves in ebb and flow.
Through laughter shared, and tears displayed,
In this ocean of us, we grow.

The cycles turn, the moon takes flight,
Pulling on hearts with gentle grace.
In deepest dark or sparkling light,
We find our way in this vast space.

Each emotion, a wave that crests,
Connecting us in ways unknown.
In every surge, our love invests,
In tides of emotions, we have grown.

Winds Carrying Familiar Hums

The breeze whispers tales of yesterday,
Carrying scents of blooming flowers.
Reminders of times that slipped away,
In every gust, the heart empowers.

Echoes of laughter float through the air,
A melody that sings to the soul.
Through paths once walked, we breathe the rare,
Winds that guide and make us whole.

Carried along, with footprints etched,
Memories dance upon the breeze.
In each soft kiss, our hearts are stretched,
United in whispers of the trees.

The familiar hums become our song,
In nature's chorus, we find our peace.
With every gust, we all belong,
In the winds of love, sweet release.

As twilight falls, the winds will change,
Yet each note lingers, sweet and clear.
Familiar hums, never strange,
In harmony, we hold each dear.

Tidal Touches

The waves whisper low, soft on the sand,
Moonlight dances, a silvery hand.
Each crest a sweet memory that sways,
In the embrace of the ocean's displays.

Footprints trace paths of those once here,
Washed away gently, like dreams we hold dear.
The tide pulls us close, then sets us adrift,
A reminder that moments are precious, a gift.

Seashells gather stories from deep below,
In every rhythm, the winds seem to blow.
Salt on the breeze, so fresh and alive,
In the pulse of the sea, our hearts come to thrive.

As dusk meets the dawn, the horizon glows,
A circle of life where the water flows.
Each wave a reminder of love's soft touch,
In the dance of the tides, we find so much.

Under the stars, where the night feels right,
We share our dreams, bathed in moon's light.
For in every splash, there's a promise anew,
In the tidal embraces, I find you.

The Language of Together

In the hush of twilight, we find our way,
Silent whispers guide us, come what may.
Each glance a word, each smile a song,
In the soft, sweet space where we both belong.

Fingers entwined, the world fades away,
In the language of hearts, we softly play.
Conversations of laughter, stories unfold,
In the warmth of your gaze, I feel bold.

Together we weave through the days and nights,
Creating a tapestry of our shared sights.
In moments of quiet, of noise and of cheer,
Our love speaks volumes that only we hear.

Every shared secret, a precious embrace,
The kindness we give, a warm, gentle grace.
In the rhythm of life, our hearts beat as one,
In the language of together, we've only begun.

So let us keep speaking in tones that unite,
In each whispered promise, in each shared light.
With laughter and love, our story is penned,
In this beautiful language that never will end.

Fireside Dialogues

By the crackling flames, we gather near,
Sharing tales, laughter, and warmth in the sphere.
The firelight dances, casting shadows bold,
In this circle of earnest, our stories unfold.

Voices raised softly, like embers take flight,
Each word a spark, glowing in the night.
Comfort in silence, in the embers that glow,
Fireside dialogues weave the warmth we bestow.

In the depths of the night, secrets take form,
Wrapped in the coziness, safe from the storm.
Life's ups and downs, all shared in the glow,
As the flames flicker softly, our bond starts to grow.

With mugs held high, we toast to the past,
To moments together that forever will last.
In the flicker and flame, our hearts intertwine,
In fireside dialogues, your love feels divine.

So let the fire burn bright, let the stories flow,
In the warmth of our laughter, together we glow.
For in this alignment of hearts and of minds,
Fireside connections are the best that one finds.

Labyrinth of Affection

In the maze of longing, paths twist and turn,
Every corner reveals, and hearts often yearn.
We wander through shadows, where love hides away,
In the labyrinth of affection, we find our way.

Each step is a promise, a choice to explore,
Whispers in silence, our spirits can soar.
Through echoes of laughter, the rattles of tears,
In this intricate dance, we shed all our fears.

With every encounter, new doorways will show,
Leading us deeper, where true feelings grow.
The twists and the turns unveil what is true,
In the labyrinth of affection, it's just me and you.

A tapestry formed from the threads of our hearts,
In the warmth of connection, each moment imparts.
As we navigate these paths, hand in hand,
In the maze of affection, together we stand.

So wander with me through this intricate scheme,
In the pathways of love, we'll build our own dream.
For in this framework, so rich and so grand,
The labyrinth of affection helps us to understand.

A Dance in the Forest of Souls

In shadows deep where whispers play,
The leaves will sway to the night's ballet.
Moonlit paths where spirits glide,
In this enchanted forest, secrets hide.

With every step, the echoes call,
As tree trunks dance, and shadows fall.
The breeze sings soft, a timeless tune,
In the heart of night, beneath the moon.

Mysteries weave through branches tall,
Each rustling leaf a silent thrall.
Nature's breath in tender embrace,
In the forest's heart, we find our place.

Around the glen, the fireflies roam,
Guiding lost shadows, finding home.
In circles drawn by ancient lore,
We sway together, forevermore.

So here we dance, in timeless grace,
Bound by the magic, in this sacred space.
Every leap holds a story untold,
In the forest of souls, where time unfolds.

Metaphors of Heartfelt Journeys

Every road, a tale to share,
Winding paths of hope and care.
Beneath the sky, we chase the sun,
In every heartbeat, journeys begun.

Mountains rise and valleys fall,
Through storms we walk, through light we call.
Each moment like a stepping stone,
In the vastness, we find our own.

With every choice, a bridge we build,
In dreams fulfilled, and fears distilled.
The map of life, a canvas wide,
Guided by stars, in grace we ride.

Silent whispers, the compass true,
Leading us onward, me and you.
Through tangled roots and fields of gold,
In shared adventures, our hearts unfold.

In the rearview, memories glow,
The love we carry will always show.
Embrace the journey, every mile,
With every step, we'll find our smile.

Ties in Motion, Never Still

In a world where moments fly,
Ties of heartstrings, never shy.
Woven bonds in laughter and tears,
In every whisper, the love endears.

With hands entwined, we sway and spin,
In the dance of life, we always win.
Through every trial, we stand as one,
Tethered tightly, when all is done.

The ebb of time, a river flows,
In tides of change, the heart still knows.
Connections hum, a vibrant thread,
In the tapestry of words unsaid.

From dawn till dusk, the journey goes,
Through shadows cast and sunshine glows.
In every heartbeat, the pulse we feel,
A bond unbroken, forever real.

So let us move, let spirits rise,
In the dance of life beneath the skies.
Together we'll chase the endless thrill,
In ties of motion, we are never still.

Resonations of Past and Present

Echoes linger from days gone by,
In whispers soft, like a gentle sigh.
Stepping stones of stories retold,
In the tapestry of memories bold.

The voices of yesteryears play clear,
In melodies that draw us near.
Present moments, a fleeting light,
In shadows cast, they mix with night.

Each heartbeat sings a timeless tune,
In the cosmic dance, like stars and moon.
The past we cherish, the present we hold,
In every heartbeat, we are consoled.

In labyrinths of time we roam,
Finding solace, finding home.
Resonations weave through our days,
In memories and dreams, the heart relays.

So let us cherish, let us explore,
The echoes of life, the evermore.
In the harmony of time's embrace,
The past and present, a sacred space.

Unbroken Circles of Being

In echoes of the ancient song,
Life dances where we all belong.
Each heartbeat a gentle refrain,
Connecting us through joy and pain.

A tapestry of shadows cast,
Woven deep, unyielding and vast.
In every circle, a spark ignites,
Guiding us through the coldest nights.

Infinite loops of love and trust,
In every moment, it's a must.
With every breath, we circle round,
In the stillness, our truth is found.

Together we rise, together we fall,
A symphony echoing through us all.
With open hands, we share the light,
In unbroken circles, we unite.

In the dance of dusk and dawn,
Every finish is a hopeful start drawn.
With gratitude, we walk this way,
In circles of being, we choose to stay.

Bridges of Breath and Heart

Across the waters, dreams take flight,
Bridges build under the silver light.
Every heartbeat echoes a song,
Binding our spirits where we belong.

With whispers soft as morning dew,
We find the strength to break right through.
In every breath, a bridge made anew,
Connecting hearts with love so true.

We walk on paths of woven fate,
Where souls entwine and celebrate.
In the silence, we share our fears,
In the laughter, we drop our tears.

Each bridge a promise, each heartbeat a spark,
Guiding us home through the shadows dark.
Together, we rise, we conquer, we play,
Bridges uniting, come what may.

In the rhythm of life, we find our way,
With bridges of breath that guide and stay.
In the bond of our hearts, we dare to believe,
Love's woven bridges, we shall receive.

Tides of Togetherness

Waves crash softly on the shore,
Bringing whispers of evermore.
In the distance, our dreams align,
In the tides, our hearts intertwine.

The ocean sings of journeys far,
Each splash a reminder of who we are.
In the ebb and flow, we find our place,
Together we dance in time and space.

With every surge, love's rhythm we feel,
In the depths of our souls, it's a sacred seal.
Through the calm and the storms, we will stand,
In the tides of togetherness, hand in hand.

As twilight descends, the stars take flight,
Guiding our hearts through the velvet night.
In the quiet, we find our way,
In the tides of love that softly sway.

The moon bathes us in silver light,
As we bask in the glow, holding tight.
With each rising tide, we'll stay the course,
In the sea of togetherness, our true source.

Fragments of Intertwined Lives

In the mosaic of moments shared,
Each fragment a story, beautifully bared.
As lives entwine in laughter and tears,
We create a tapestry woven through years.

The past and present dance in a swirl,
In the fabric of time, our spirits unfurl.
Each memory a thread, vibrant and bright,
In the shadows and light, we take flight.

With whispers of hope, we find our way,
In fragments of love, come what may.
Together we stitch, through joy and strife,
Creating a quilt of our intertwined life.

Through every heartache, through every smile,
In the journey together, we walk each mile.
With open arms, we embrace the chance,
In the dance of existence, we find romance.

As stars align in a cosmic embrace,
In fragments of lives, we find our place.
With each new dawn, we'll rise and thrive,
In the melody of dreams, we come alive.

Milton Keynes UK
Ingram Content Group UK Ltd.
UKHW020826141124
451073UK00007BA/150

9 789916 865873